*Naming the Dawn*

THE AFRICA LIST

*Naming the Dawn*

ABDOURAHMAN A. WABERI

Translated by Nancy Naomi Carlson

LONDON NEW YORK CALCUTTA

www.bibliofrance.in

The work is published with the support of the Publication
Assistance Programmes of the Institut français

**Seagull Books, 2018**

Originally published in French as Abdourahman A. Waberi,
*Mon nom est aube*

© Abdourahman A. Waberi
Published by arrangement with Agence litteraire Astier-Pécher

First published in English translation by Seagull Books, 2018
English translation © Nancy Naomi Carlson, 2017

ISBN   978 0 8574 2 546 1

**British Library Cataloguing-in-Publication Data**
A catalogue record for this book is available from the British
Library.

Typeset by Seagull Books, Calcutta, India
Printed and bound by Maple Press, York, Pennsylvania, USA

*For Souleymane Bachir Diagne*

## Contents

*Foreword*

And I find myself absolutely enchanted—bewildered too—by the friendship reflected in this dedication, which makes me, in a way, the first recipient of this collection titled *Naming the Dawn*. Which I begin my reading with the reminder from the poet that 'the law is not the path that leads to the source'. To understand the poetic link that ties together the 'law' and the way that leads (back) to the source is, among infinite possibilities, to realize that sharia, by which is usually meant the 'law', is in both its first and final meaning the 'path that leads the herd to the watering hole where it can drink'. Thus, the poet tells us first that in 'the path that leads to the source' it's not about the 'law' but about being born 'with the passion for truth and beauty bound to the heart'. This passion is what is being offered here in simple, profound words, 'seemingly no big deal', an invitation to share a quiet alliance. Nothing too loud: only an invitation to the spiritual exercise of tasting, then chewing. Taste the apple. Chew on the Book that 'was sent down from the heavens'. Yes, within these poems that sing of the path to truth and beauty, it is all about savour.

*Souleymane Bachir Diagne*

*This night is full of peace*
*until dawn appears*

Al-Qadr, Koran

*Living Soul*

*The worst thing the Eternal can do to his little creatures*
*is to let them fulfil their dreams.*
*For their dreams are always too cramped.*

Christiane Singer

*O Men*


the white-haired child is there, upright in the mire
a son of Adam seeking the Orient within
seeing himself in the eyes of the pack
that combs the countryside, spurred on by brass
    horns

his fortune has no bounds

he pores over matter
which unnerves his world
especially the timid ones striding on ibis legs,
the uncertain, the mute on the towpath to fords

crowds who nod
in front of their dull screens
have nothing for him
but scorpion darts

they swear to place on the chopping block
his ephebic head and his slender neck

a miracle if he's from this world
it would come from the force of his frailty
a river from Al-Kawthar
regaining its strength in adversity's grip

a torrent that rises, turns into pure azure blue
that winds among the stars
covets in such clear water
the light of its stellar twin

*May My Right Hand Forget Me*


when somebody knocks on my door
it's God asking for shelter

make yourself at home and recite for me please
a sacred song from your native land
you who live in exile in the West
and the wistful lines of your ancient poem
in what language do you speak to mortals in groves

we're promised a Garden of Eden high above
a space where life fills the nave's flesh with breath
from every evergreen tree

you who dwell on earth: if you still don't know
    what's hidden in roots
or the hunger of innards
take care of your body
as if it were a lab
an artist's workshop of every moment in time
to show you how life evolved
the myriad tricks of sap and bee
his other name: not the random act but the gift

his acrid flame grabs
the misfits who wriggle like locusts

on grills
continues its round of myrrh
it's a private war lodged in the bowels
provincial interior towns

the stone is rolled away, the sun has risen
there where the rabble reels and flails
for lack of a branch

failed light!

may my right hand forget me
if I turn a deaf ear to your guttural prayer
sprung from deep beneath the arc
where your solar plexus burns

*Slantwise*


write the war not here
no longer here
by degrees
in bursts on the winged beats of words
in place of the stranger who comes

slantwise as well
how many stories swell under my quill
there's no excuse—just rust lying in wait
erosion of conscience
concealed by the deepest gloom

why on earth try
why on earth try

time's up

*Touchstones*


massaging the wounded men
their bodies in dire distress
washing holding
feeding clothing calming
I came to discover the oneness of their being
to make a dent in the human clock
the crested line jolted by emotions
on a mountain range they say the shortest route
goes from one peak to the next


I trace the body's trail
with my eyes closed
and reach
vertebra after vertebra
the delicate tip of their soul
as I tread on the holy land of bones


there's always an ounce of sense in their delusions
a hint of youth within their screams
I've come to realize you cannot touch
without being touched
suffering all around but still this: rapture upon rapture
I too am ablaze
here and here—
yes, here

*Juvenescence*

what is true

bloomed among new nascent buds
from this moment able to breathe
like the doum palm's seed
the sap that drives an ecstatic rite
where it's Sunday every day

the aorta's clot
the slight sidereal wind
the atom's unctuous birth
the élan vital that knocks over all in its path
cornered, it opens the way that can't be denied
the unmapped trail
for the green snake that slithers ahead alone
further still from its molted skin
to the solar star's great dismay
no longer poised to instantly imbue it with life

*Of a Salvo in Its Shrine*

real thirst is a grace
thank God not everyone thirsts
for eau-de-vie and the absolute
not everyone craves
cocktails of ocean and liquid nitrogen's smoke

tired of being buried alive I veer toward ventures
that deeply move me, make me vibrate inside
even if I must live a dozen lives in a row
to reach Thuraya's stars

I catch sight of the spire that cuts the light of day
its igneous energy new like the rose of Shiraz
I bless the union of heaven infused in my blood
from the depths of my breath
give thanks to the zither's thin voice that counts, rosary-style
causes and cures
the lamp that drives away gloom
recourse to poetry's truth
root and bloom
bee and honeyed brood
war and truce
shepherd and flock
written word and prayer
silence and tune

the beloved's wild silk
in its shrine
surrounded by peace

*At the Botanical Garden*


building up trust in the vigour
of friendship, I see you
through my eyelids
near the very end of the path
as you come into view in the flesh
your feet lashed by the ermine-white snow

in your hand
the old rosette of thorns
the Bedouins used long ago
to card the wool of sheep
and in the pocket over your heart
below your chest's meridian
the straw-yellow card
with words of the daily verse

the prayer is sent to the sky
proclamation made by your eye today
or tomorrow perhaps by your ear
in league with the drop of water which always knew
        to expect
by some miracle
all of the battering sea

but you aim to hold at bay
self-concern
and all the russet-haired beasts, young wild boars or
        sea wolves
creatures with claws, scales and fangs
covered with blood or soot
all your repressed devils
loquacious and quarrelsome
ready to bound from your chest
to violently bounce off walls
on the opposite side
at the slightest annoyance

you will flee their flaming banners
their myriad teeth marks
the path is measured step by step
by a single instant's quality
seized from the contours of its darkness
dimensions matching in secret
the ring of its good deeds

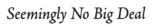

*Seemingly No Big Deal*

*Our single great achievement is our life,*
*especially our death.*

Louis Massignon

*Chasing after Death*


estranged from yourself
you failed to see in your dreams
the trees that offered their leathery leaves
to the sleepy pupils of our eyes
the sky rich with shimmering sea urchins
the ocean keeping the beat since yesterday's dawn
you never had time to adjust your mount
braving back-and-forth bursts of wind
never could sweep through your daily rounds
just some dusting here and there
it's grizzly grey outside
which makes us light up from within
the smallest thing will brighten your household again
if you're back on track
it's thanks to all of us here
to our persistent dream to grow in time

*Bottle*


to stay calm when faced with a surging thirst
or succumb on the spot before sustaining
the rain of jabs below the belt

no, it's really hard
I can better resist
more or less
when alone
I'm afraid to call home
I feel a sudden urge
to maintain my distance
to keep them from telling me problems
which once again
I won't know how to solve on my own

far from Peter and Paul
and the daunting crowd
I hang over the lion's maw
tonight the bench is keeping me
upright
I'm getting drunk on disgusting wine
I'll call tomorrow, I swear

*Yes, but What Do You Say about This, My Daughter?*


fill the doorway to your mind
get out into summer's brightness and warmth
leave the slime and abyss behind
put on some music in cut-time
it's the hour to roar
to once again find

the secret of joy—
I'll be truthful with you—
is before your eyes
listen to birds sing

in the setting sun facing
Aleppo's citadel
have a good time
see you later, my love

*Language of Birds*


*iqra*
in the name of the God on High, recite
psalmody now
the crucial syllables
creation sung at sight
rising again to the surface
your beating heart
supplies the rhythm
nothing you need to devise
everything's come before
it's all here


the seed, the bark, the crown and the thorns
the errant eros of time
life in death
death in life
the source and the sea
the dove perched on your grave

*iqra*
the elusive peace
in Mesopotamia
Syria's consuming fire
the moment becoming eternity
the ball that whirls

the past won't belie its present
it's all here
already present

wholly alive
impermanent too
in days ahead
memory's daze
the creation
the arrows and bow of his everlasting surprise

*Daily Awakening*


he's reportedly distant above
on a cloud
and we're like a new bird
perched on our hill
compelled by the duty to love
the delight of painting life black

my own blood pulses
a splendid part
makes me simply a man among men
an elder without a crown
a bulbous stone in the wilderness
Adam mired in the mud
is blind to the shooting star
the seed that bursts out of humus
the lotus that blooms in manure where old Job made
     his honey
then pried open the Buddhas' lips
on the brink of jouissance

they say he's a major no-show
up there by himself
they say there's a hitch
next time

he too will leave behind his skin
the ancient tortoise slow to evolve
with a swallow resolved to ride on his back

*Reader*


she lives barefoot
in the middle of nowhere
a mere nothing makes her smile
makes her blow a fuse
what a disaster, she utters under her breath
my stomach's in knots from a headache
      reaching my glottis

two clouds later
she's still butt-sliding down
gliding through pockets of air
serene amid unbounded abandon's plumes

before the poem ends
and the minutes offend
for sure
the rain will be dense

here in chair or bed she spends
most of the days of her life
and most of the hours of her day
pondering silence

at night
she listens
to a young doum palm
grow even more green

*O Mother*


in my memory
my mother went to put on her white mourning dress
I've stashed this image away
in the drawer of timeworn things

my mouth on fire
like Jacob
I limped from a wrenched hip
for having crossed swords with the angel
elbowed my way through when I saw the ford
the sandglass is launched, course set for the
     motherwort sea,

Mother, you're no longer here
except in the yesterday and tears of my song
none will restore your life's salt
your smile's gold
your line's blood
if not for my murmur's touch

*Absence*


what I know—in sum, scarcely much—
and what I search for converge
in these days of dearth

the one who watches over the house is gone
giving a tug on the invisible's cord
this friend in wisdom has passed

it's not the big ball of dough
but the pinch of yeast that makes the bread
many are those who find
the sublime in the daily grind
by beginning to grow as they shuffle along their way

*Sepia*


together, they shared *du thé et des oranges*
*tea and oranges*
and sweetly made love
in a folk ballad's perfect calm

from this embrace
the only trace is a single image, just one

guitar and long hair completely spent
on the shore of the past
and beneath our feet
the crack's invisible river
soaking up in its grooves
the capricious contours of tune

*Vanity*

it's easy to fritter your life away
bit by bit
without even being aware

I desire and deserve it all
the odd arithmetic of ignorance
I fear misfortune

with all the force of my life
yet I run toward it
mouth and arms open

the din of the herd is more ingrained
than each individual's joy

*It's a Girl*


I hold baby close
and my heart floods all over again
grateful for what I behold

braced against headwinds and years
the layout of life
child's play, art
giving birth
laboring on with no guarantees
the road to Kabul
the body's unfinished design
the racing breath
an entire lifetime's froth

for this hope
I lend my flesh, my pen and my bones

*Yesterdaze*


riddles written in sand
soaring syllables sprung from the oldest of times
imprinted on everyone's lips

parable helping you see the present day's texture
beyond the mob and its thousand backs of necks

the believer bent in half by prayer is infused
by the mineral signs of intoned words of praise
like the treasures brought to life
by the mighty Euphrates and Tigris rivers
*dikr*


words sprinkle down
into the ear's retreat
impermanent poems
reluctant
it's true, to follow the winged steed
five times across the mountains

once you conquer your fear
you may catch in mid-air the prayers

that fervent pilgrims fling to the sky
for themselves but expressly for others
go pray with them
shoulder to shoulder
and not row by row
like comrades in arms in the muck

you'll rid your mind of both the fay
and her brother the djinn
escaped from their flask
who feed on random effluvia

unite firebrand with eaglewood
the evil eye will keep away
trembling more than a reed
tormented more than the robber repenting at death's door
when he doesn't know if he'll be swept away by the last
    sudden downpour
wild as can be
or struck down on the spot
bludgeoned to death from the judgement of peers

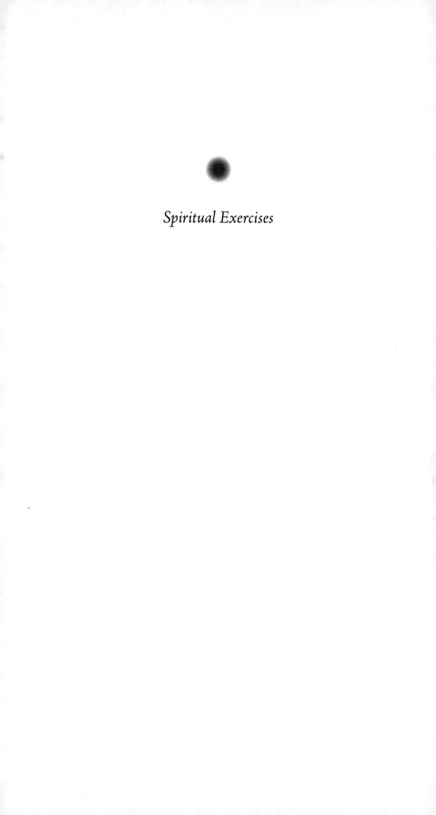

*Spiritual Exercises*

*A star is placed in the sky for each one of us, far enough away so that our mistakes can never tarnish it.*

Christian Bobin

*Access*


my revolt was in vain
silence gives me its breast
its music
simple, sincere
flows like ablution water
that preludes the call to prayer

the words born on the lips of the Guide
transport knowledge's wine
by the barrel
I pursued this elixir as soon as the sun
lovingly drank up the mist before my eyes
from temple to temple
and soon the moon out of pity's sake gave me a pebble
orphaned from quarterly vigil

a shaft of light precedes me

and my back
in turn
clumsily reflects
the slender harp-shaped form of the being
who kindly walked
in my faltering steps

my revolt was in vain
no regrets
the journey is long
tomorrow I'll set off again
with dawn slung over my shoulder

*Aura*


a pair of shabby shoes
resting on the threshold of a farm
in a painting by Van Gogh
bears witness to the missing peasant
vanished, snatched by seductive powers
of Chagall's skies

swiftly somewhere
someone takes wing
an angel slips into the frame
a tuft of dove feathers, a bucket—no, a coat
to warm
the face of the one not here

we all know
the presence and spirit of anyone
seen as a whole
creates charisma's oval

*Anchor*

o man of wind with headstrong ways
more intent than your shadow
my brother, what are you after
so prized at the end of the trail you follow
    with lowered eyes—
the smoke screen of status quo your excuse
nothing is pressing for you or your kind—
at hand for your little pilgrimage:
your acupoint pathways mapping meridian flows

*Turn Away from the Cramped Attentional Tunnel*


go pluck the dangling apple and take special note
of the magic enclosed in the hand whose fingers
curl in the shape of a firm pear, of the raised arm,
of the shoulder foreseeing the fruit's fall

of the head that slides on its axis in order to let the
    gaze
drift to the side
the whole body is set in motion,
from toes to the top of the skull,
absorbs all things while it listens with every orifice
pores and skin
you'll wholeheartedly welcome each miniscule move
from its earliest impulse to when it blends
into the all-encompassing gesture

abandon the old body riddled with quirks

we are beings in constant change
the train of your thoughts will trace its endless route


come back my brother
come back to the apple, sensations
produced on the spot

pupil of eye drooling ahead of palate
nose hairs yielding like wheat in a gust of wind
idea of apple about to be chewed
journey of juice from mouth to throat

come back to the hand
to the main intention
by day or by night
moor your attention there like a ship to the quay
know that you need eyes in order to slaughter
others to love, rush around or die
and hands to bear the train of the bridal gown
ask the bee for her retina's secrets
ten minutes or ten years down the road
under the guidance of breath


your hand will teach you the way to make piercing
     vision yours
to revive your gazelle mind

o son of yesterday's haste
now more still than your shadow
you'll remain eternal
constantly ageless and new
like the one who meditates, keeping centred
calm

o son of dawn, each time there's a need you'll
        describe
the intentional tunnel without raising your voice
nor backing down

in a clear voice as humble as clay
you'll declare that there's nothing concealed
that everything's here before our eyes
the past, the present life and the one to come

you'll summon peace to the shoulders
of both your lifelong friend and the peppy sparrow
        that sings
on Gabriel's wing

*Ascension*


draped in a white shroud
your feet a mirage
here you are, man of clay, on the side
of the mountain of light
specks of dust rise in your wake
the blessed grotto right at the end of the climb
will shelter your tired shepherd's bones

this is it
you smile at the angels with two, three or four wings

for a moment
one brief moment
the angels' face and yours are identical
twin brothers—two sides of a paper dream

*Asceticism*


release what's been repressed
scars of wounds, strokes of fate
soot of fears welling up in the bosom of Eve
we keep a scared or disgraced child
asleep deep down in our guts
weeping returns with evening despair
red-faced the newborn mewls as soon as Mamma's
    scent
slips away from his grasp

baby is a big lake
the tears that fill it make no ripples
you will sense all the mud-covered dreams on the
    prowl
amassed in this life
and in lives of the women and men
whose projected shadows we remain
we endure as a speck of infinity
beings who've wandered in circles
around our pastures for such a long time

at the end of a lengthy season of patience
footprints and strife disappear like morning dew
the union's lotus reveals its promise
on the ashes of the past

effect nuzzles cause in a loving embrace
and renewed
you beam at the sun of peace found again

*Pavement Struggle*


with my eagle eye open wide
I track the autumn or summer leaf
curled into itself
torn from its native tree
parading its solitude along the pavement across the
    street

teasing it rests a while then resumes its rush
a young woman carrying half a baguette under her
    arm
leaves the baker's shop with small measured steps
drunk on wind
the leaf flings itself at her shinbone
blind to the passer-by's muscular strength

it appears, as my eagle eye makes known,
that all is settled on the spot
that the leaf is born into the world
to display its secret to you

but lo and behold it gives
the passer-by's leg the slip
with clear-cut determination, opens the path
for it's sacrilege
counters my eagle eye

to keep to the beaten track
even when you're a small leaf
engulfed by vacuity's vast sea

*A Shroud for All Time*


an old saying goes that we live out our days
clad in a shroud thrown over one shoulder

no need to be God
to confirm the mystical world of the spirit and angels
heaven and hell
the almond tree in full bloom
and all the rare people who speak on behalf of
    Ineffable truths

to us all
we were given the gift to know
that secrets must exist for mystery's sake

to be born with the passion for truth and beauty
    bound to the Heart

to us all
the holy days of eternity
life force entrusted to what can't be seen

*Wager*


if the belly barely conceals the guts
if fingers serve as adornments for hands
if zodiac signs remain close-mouthed
if bones that propel us across the earth's mud
are only water mixed with a little ether
if picking up our own manure is a great lesson learnt
in the same way that ceasing to split 'pure' from 'vile'
is still the path that brings clarity back
if giving the leper a kiss is the best way to make
our internal mirror shine
then Lord do not make of me
this shadow who draws its substance
from someone else's breath
I'll proceed straight ahead
to seal in a single weft
my deeds and myself

*Bees*


enraptured narcissus petals bend
in search of their own reflection
the diurnal round spins
in search of its other half
Majnun's lonely eyes
trace all of Layla's tracks
the wolf dozing in me
sleeps with only one eye

*Wedding*


through Heaven's gaze that comes to fall
level with soil
and through a dense silence winding
the length of the smouldering shade
the Holy Book is where Heaven and Earth converse
in silent devotion
through reason's sieve
firmly stuck in the earth
in the realm of the Heart


with no ban or command
other than seeding itself through repeated prayers
the complete Book contained in the mouth
choreographs, exhales
propels into orbit
the jazzed-up language of bees

*In a Naked Voice*


I keep small seeds inside my cheeks
shards of rock below my palate
here's your book, my mother hands me the Koran
hold this treasure close to your chest to protect you
from every trap and donkey kick
life never ceases to place on our path


I recite the Fatiha one last time


one last time I ask my immured father
why he can't see me
why one day the plant no longer pierces the earth
in time we hope his reply
won't matter any more
one day we'll no longer go
rolling this question along the road

*Détente*


it's the outer child who speaks
to the inner child
who awakens, smiles or cries out of view
concealed from the eyes that witnessed his birth


writing makes the carnal come alive


in his fist the child grips paper and pencil
and plumbs the language of blooms and silent things
slips through sand
in a flash comes back as flood
legs bowed
head bent
howling with laughter, racing about
a tiny spade in his hand
and in each pupil of his eyes
an entire realm

*O Rising Sun*


my mother's voice: a handful of salt
when I think of tomorrow and all I will do
afraid of a full day's frenzy of work
I'd rather postpone to the following day
it's more humane

I call it a missed glance
the one that fails to touch the passer-by

I leave mind games behind
wanting to grasp smoke
you exhaust yourself in vain
wanting to swallow the moon
you choke on the slightest bite
I search no more
all is already mine

*Sitting*


the warrior on the wire of his breath
mirrors the calm of the cherry leaf
the peace of those who sleep in mountain air
the blade of the sword by which men live

through intercession of the tree
that hangs from ravine's edge
the divine connects with the muddy man
born from a lump of clay
tucked away in the cove of silence

lost in the noisy maze of his own time
he gives names to so many things
witnessed by bare-breasted stars

*Axis*


just a cluster of cells
set upright again by the sun of a glance
forcing open the lock of living things

just a gift from others
lifted by love
storming the sleeping citadel
blowing the trumpets of Jericho

just a present from Providence and chance
epiphany snatched like a kiss
before crumbling
in turn
into dust

in truth
I tell you
just a clandestine gift
midday's child
and abandon's ecstatic delight

*Advent*

the colour of water takes on the shade of its vessel
the shade of dawn is the same as the call
the small forehead cross on the first day of Lent
announces the season's fasting days
want is not a lack but ineffable surfeit
poking big holes in consumption's short coat
confining to bed
the totem tuckered out from a stroll in the mall

the colour of water is not the same as the latest cos-
    metic trick
or the prod of my spoken words
approaching a stranger
on days of silence
to help evoke an absent One

*Not a Day Will Pass*


baby wriggles and giggles by turns
philosophical, he ponders
what did I look like before my parents' birth

in his mouth, the entire Book sent down from the
 heavens
and in his chest an ember glows
waving its flame since yesterday's wee hours

and in his little hands a sun of psalm
puts on a show for the overflowing cistern of his
 tears
which succumbs in the face-off

neither anchor nor helm
but the port if need be
and now baby takes off, at once autonomous
still sustained the following day by seraphic breath,
 he unveils
the clump of clay of the coming world

a hand pressed into ours
a flutter of wings
the shade of a tree with a good place to rest

an endless sprawling beach
an interior landscape—austere and concise—
a reading room's worried hardwood floor
silence revealing such lofty designs to the Word

*Faerie*

once
I offered the world my nihilistic facade
unbounded harsh words
a bouquet of thorns reserved to keep
intact a bundle of wounds
the wheel of mankind has reached its final station
we must, I proposed in a loud cry, record its swansong
    before labour's end

now that I've felt the sense of shelter
here and there in the shifting world
in the age of digital disembodiment
adrift in its night

I intend to welcome face to face or side by side
the unruly mules and the fuming scorpions lost
in the back streets of their madness
barely disposed these days to decipher the Book
    of Creation and reach the cape of great hope
for we know they, too, have a heart
craving
closeness

the law isn't the path that leads to the source
a century-old misconception

that probably suits the many
who gallop at breakneck speed
kaffiyehs askew
whiskers smooth and smiles in retreat
did the Arabs not know the word sky means
nature in Chinese and conversely
that energy flow is conferred on us then withdrawn
not one ounce of drama there
nor pause
in the four seasons of mortal life

the parting of seas comes to pass in a breath
the great and austere philosophical texts are no more
of use than the flash bursting forth from the poem
bouquet of brief quotes
delightfully funny anecdotes, short accounts
inviting us to let things bend with the curve
and embrace the swimmer's movement borne by the
     swell
that leads to the source or that of the novice
     launched
into endless probes of the peregrine letter renewing
     itself
in the Beloved's shade

## The Hoopoe

*o reader, my brother, my sister, savour this*
*one final tale—enjoy!*

one day
a distant country—land of incense, spices and herbs
a country acquainted with shifting
    existence
a poet went to a marketplace
he bought a handmade cage
    of wood
and lengths of string
to house there—in fact
a paper bird

*Translator's Notes*

PAGE 5. *O Men*

Al-Kawthar is the name of a chapter in the Koran, and also refers to a river in Paradise.


PAGE 12. *Of a Salvo in Its Shrine*

Thuraya is the Arabic name for the constellation of the Pleiades.


PAGE 24. *Language of Birds*

*Iqra* is an Arabic word that means 'recite!' or 'read!' and is the first word of the Koran.


PAGE 32. *Sepia*

This poem references lyrics by Leonard Cohen.


PAGE 35. *Yesterdaze*

*Dikr* refers to an Islamic form of devotion whereby the worshipper repeats short utterances glorifying God. The 'winged steed', associated with celestial ascension, refers to Buraq, the mythical horse of the Prophet Muhammad.

PAGE 53. *A Shroud for All Time*

The first stanza refers to the Ihram attire worn by Muslims while on pilgrimage to Mecca.


PAGE 55. *Bees*

Majnun and Layla were star-crossed lovers in a story written in eleventh-century Arabia.


PAGE 57. *In a Naked Voice*

The Fatiha, containing seven verses, is the opening prayer of the Koran, and is typically recited at least seventeen times each day.

*Acknowledgements*

I am grateful to Catherine Maigret Kellogg for her generosity in providing invaluable comments for early drafts of this manuscript.

Many thanks to the editors of the following literary journals in which versions of these translations first appeared:

*The Arkansas International*: 'Sitting'

*ArLiJo*: 'Bees', 'Juvenescence'

*Catamaran*: 'Sepia'

*The Chattahoochee Review*: 'O Rising Sun', 'Turn Away from the Cramped Attentional Tunnel'

*Ezra*: 'Advent', 'O Mother', 'Pavement Struggle', 'Yesterdaze'

*Harvard Review*: 'Absence', 'Aura', 'Chasing After Death'

*The Ilanot Review*: 'Reader'

*Image*: 'May My Right Hand Forget Me', 'O Men', 'A Shroud for All Time'

*Mid-American Review*: 'Anchor', 'At the Botanical Garden', 'Détente', 'Faerie', 'Of a Salvo in Its Shrine'

*Peacock Journal*: ' Axis', 'Daily Awakening', 'Slantwise', 'It's a Girl' and 'Yes, but What Do You Say about This, My Daughter?'

*Plume*: 'Vanity'

*Poetry Flash*: 'Touchstones', 'Wedding'

*Poetry International:* 'Bottle'

*Prairie Schooner:* 'The Hoopoe', 'In Plain Speech', 'Wager'

*ROAR:* 'Asceticism', 'Language of Birds', 'Not a Day Will Pass'

*Waxwing:* 'Access', 'Ascension'

*Nancy Naomi Carlson*